Cesar
Chavez

Cesar Chavez, president of the United Farm Workers (UFW), leads a group of pickets in San Francisco, California, to urge a boycott of lettuce in 1979.

JUNIOR ■ WORLD ■ BIOGRAPHIES

Cesar Chavez

BRUCE W. CONORD

CHELSEA JUNIORS

a division of CHELSEA HOUSE PUBLISHERS

Chelsea House Publishers
EDITOR-IN-CHIEF: Remmel Nunn
MANAGING EDITOR: Karyn Gullen Browne
COPY CHIEF: Mark Rifkin
PICTURE EDITOR: Adrian G. Allen
ART DIRECTOR: Maria Epes
ASSISTANT ART DIRECTOR: Howard Brotman
MANUFACTURING DIRECTOR: Gerald Levine
SYSTEMS MANAGER: Lindsey Ottman
PRODUCTION MANAGER: Joseph Romano
PRODUCTION COORDINATOR: Marie Claire Cebrián

JUNIOR WORLD BIOGRAPHIES

SENIOR EDITOR: Kathy Kuhtz

Staff for CESAR CHAVEZ
EDITORIAL ASSISTANT: Danielle Janusz
PICTURE RESEARCHER: Diana Gongora
SENIOR DESIGNER: Marjorie Zaum
COVER ILLUSTRATION: Steven Parton

First Printing

1 3 5 7 9 8 6 4 2

Library of Congress Cataloging-in-Publication Data
Conord, Bruce W.
  Cesar Chavez/Bruce W. Conord.
    p.   cm.—(Junior world biographies)
  Includes index.
  Summary: A biography of the union activist who led the struggle of migrant
farm workers for better working conditions.
  ISBN 0-7910-1757-5
  1. Chavez, Cesar, 1927–   —Juvenile literature. 2. Labor leaders—United
States—Biography—Juvenile literature. 3. Trade-unions—Migrant
agricultural laborers—United States—History—Juvenile literature.
[1. Chavez, Cesar, 1927– . 2. Labor leaders. 3. Mexican Americans—
Biography. 4. Migrant labor.] I. Title. II. Series.
HD6509.C48C66 1992   91-22169
331.88′13′092—dc20   CIP
[B]   AC

Contents

In 1966, striking grape pickers in California protest low wages, poor living conditions, and unfair hiring practices. Chavez's union, the National Farm Workers Association, organized the march.

1

Drama
in the Desert

From two small slits in the side of the truck, Cesar Chavez could see the guards. It was the summer of 1965, and he was locked in the back of a truck with several farm workers and two clergymen. With the hot California sun beating down on the dusty truck, the temperature rose to about 100 degrees Fahrenheit. The men inside had no water to drink, and the hot, dry air made them feel like they could not breathe.

The armed guards had been hired by the farm's owners to keep Chavez and his farm workers union away from the people picking grapes in the vineyard. Members of the union went on strike to try to get the owners to improve the laborers' working conditions.

Chavez and the others had been walking on the dirt road that led into the fields when the six guards appeared and pushed them into the back of the truck. Now they were trapped inside and could die in the burning heat.

Four hours later, the guards took them to a labor camp where *migrant workers* lived while working on the farm. Migrant workers travel from farm to farm, planting, weeding, or picking the crops. Often, whole families, including young children, worked in the fields.

Many families had to live in filthy conditions. They had no running water or indoor toilets. Some families stayed in windowless one-room shacks with dirt floors. Other shacks, made of metal, seemed like ovens in the hot sun. But most families lived in tents, which were surrounded by mud whenever it rained.

At the camp, the guards made Chavez and the others sit for two hours before the police came. When the sheriff's deputies from the nearby town of Borrego Springs arrived, they carried heavy chains.

"Look, what is that?" one of the clergymen asked Chavez. "I wonder what they want them for? Maybe some desperadoes [criminals]."

"No," Chavez answered. "It's for us."

"Oh, Cesar, they wouldn't do that!"

"Sure, they'll do it. You wait and see."

Chavez was right. The deputies arrested them. They shackled the two clergymen and Chavez by their wrists and ankles, then chained them to each other. At the jail, the deputies searched Chavez to make sure he did not have any hidden weapons. That night Chavez had to sleep on a mattress on the floor. The police were trying to frighten him so that his union would stop organizing the local workers.

But Cesar Chavez was not afraid of their threats. His union, the *National Farm Workers Association (NFWA)*, was growing stronger every day. He believed his union could help the migrant laborers who picked fruits and vegetables in California.

Nearly half the fruits and vegetables eaten in the United States are grown in California. Most California farms are large, with thousands of acres of crops. This farmland is owned by very rich families or giant corporations, such as United Brands, which imports Chiquita brand bananas, and Purex, makers of bleach. These growers are in *agribusiness*—they combine agriculture and business. The growers also have a lot of influence in local political matters.

But Cesar Chavez understood firsthand what hard times could mean to a family of farm laborers. He had been a migrant worker himself, working right alongside his family in the fields. He knew the pain caused by bending over a short-handled hoe all day long. Many times he and his family had very little to eat.

If he and the union could change the system of farm labor, they would then be able to gain decent working conditions and better pay for the migrant workers. But change like that would prove to be very difficult. Chavez would need courage and strength from his own faith in God and from his family, because he was about to do something that others before him had tried to do—but had failed.

This 1947 photograph of Juana and Librado Chavez, Cesar's parents, was taken at a ranch near San Jose, California.

CHAPTER

2
Losing
the Farm

Lying in bed in the moonlight, Cesar and his younger brother Richard could see shapes of faces in the shadows on the walls and ceiling of the adobe house. As they lay there wide awake, they created stories from their imagination. This childhood memory is one of the many happy times Cesar remembers when he thinks about life on his grandfather's farm. But for his parents, those days were not so cheerful.

Cesar Chavez had been named for his grandfather, Cesario. Papa Chayo, as the family called Cesario, had come to the United States and sent for his family in 1888. He had fled from a Mexican farm, where he had been treated like a slave, when he stood up for another man's rights. He was afraid that he would be harshly punished for siding with the man, so he decided to escape to the United States.

As a small boy, Cesar would hear about his grandfather's escape many times. He and his brother would listen at night to other stories, including descriptions of the Mexican Revolution and of their uncles' experiences fighting against inequality. Cesar also heard stories about cave-ins and accidents in the mines, where many of his relatives had worked. His relatives told stories in which they believed their survival had been a miracle, and they credited the miracle to their strong faith in God.

After Cesar's grandfather had saved enough money, he sent for his wife and their 14 children. Cesar's father, Librado, was only two years old at the time. The family settled in the North Gila Valley, along the Colorado River in Arizona. Librado grew up to be a strong, handsome man, nearly six feet tall, with large hands. He worked on the farm even after he married Juana Estrada. Cesar's mother was a tiny, pretty woman with long black hair. Librado and Juana bought a grocery store in the valley, in Yuma, and it was there that Cesar was born on March 31, 1927.

During the 1930s, the U.S. economy collapsed and millions of people were out of work. This period in American history is called the Great Depression. Many farmers lost their land because they could not afford to pay taxes or to grow crops. Other farmers' lands were no longer fertile on account of a severe drought in the Southwest.

Because many of Librado's relatives were unemployed, he gave them credit in his store. When Librado was cheated out of some land by his neighbor in a business deal, he borrowed money to buy the land back. As his business grew worse, Librado could not pay back the loan. The store and the land had to be sold. The whole family returned to Papa Chayo's adobe house, where they lived in one big room. There was no running water or electricity on the farm.

Cesar had to walk a long way to school. He did not like school very much because he felt the teachers were mean. He could not speak English well and was often punished for speaking Spanish.

At home, his father was stern but affectionate. Even though he worked long hours, Librado created little cars from sardine cans and taught the boys how to make toy tractors from wooden spools of thread.

Cesar's mother gave the children big hugs and kisses. No matter how poor the Chavez family was, Juana believed in helping others who were less fortunate. Every year, on the birthday of her patron saint, she found a needy person to help. (A patron saint is a person's guardian saint, the

saint a person prays to for protection or help.)
Often, she brought home hoboes to feed. Juana
never took anything in return for her kindness,
and Cesar thought that her generosity was a beautiful custom.

She also gave Cesar *consejos*, which means
"advice" in Spanish, and Spanish *dichos*, or say-
ings, that had a great effect on him. Many of these
dichos and consejos were about solving personal
problems without using violence. A typical one
was: "It's best to turn the other cheek. God gave
you senses like eyes and mind and tongue, and
you can get out of anything." Her favorite dicho
was "It takes two to fight, and one can't do it
alone." His mother firmly believed in nonviolence.

"When I was young I didn't realize the
wisdom in her words," Chavez later recalled, "but
it has been proved to me so many times since."

Cesar helped his father with chores on the
farm and learned all about growing crops. Times
were bad, and there was very little money coming

in from the crops the Chavezes grew. Librado paid the doctor's bill for the birth of Cesar's sister, Vicky, with a truckload of watermelon.

The Chavez family needed cash, however, to pay the taxes they owed on the farm. When the Chavezes could not pay the tax, the land was sold at an auction. (An auction is a public sale in which things are sold to the person who offers to pay the most money.) Soon after they lost the farm, a bulldozer came and knocked down all the trees, filled in the water canal, and ripped down the corral. Ten-year-old Cesar watched the destruction of his grandfather's property and became very angry.

Librado Chavez packed his family into their old car and headed toward California. They had some relatives there and hoped to find work. Cesar's family dreamed of saving enough money to buy back their farm.

When the Chavezes arrived in California, they discovered that 300,000 poor and hungry people had already come there to find work, too.

Many of these people were also farmers. Some had lost their land during the Great Depression.

Because there were more workers than there was work, the California growers were able to pay less for the labor they needed done.

Into this system came the hardworking and proud Chavez family. For Cesar, the experiences and the hardships of this new life would give him a strong desire to help other people, as his family had before him.

But migrant families found that it was almost impossible to find work without the help of *labor contractors*. One of a labor contractor's jobs was to make sure that there was always cheap labor for the grower. Often, rumors about finding good jobs in another town caused whole families to drive all day or night to that town, only to discover that the crop had already been harvested.

Frequently, the contractors decided who would work and who would not. Some workers had to buy their job with a bribe. There were many dishonest contractors getting rich at the expense of the migrant laborers. Sometimes they even charged the workers for the water they drank while harvesting in the hot sun. Many labor contractors made money by cheating the workers when they weighed their pickings at the end of the day. For example, a contractor might claim that the scale read 89 pounds, when the load actually weighed 112 pounds. The contractors kept

Farm workers use short-handled hoes to thin young plants, such as beets, lettuce, and celery. The workers have to move slowly up and down the long rows of plants and are constantly bent over at the waist while they work.

the difference in the sum that was paid for the load for themselves.

The Chavez family drove on to San Jose for the 1939 cherry-picking season and settled in a *barrio*, which means "neighborhood" in Spanish. But to the poor people who lived there, barrio really meant "slum." It was called Sal Si Puedes— Get Out If You Can.

Every day, the Chavez family went to the farms in the area to look for work. Workers were paid for their pickings by the bushel basket or hamper, or by weight. This manner of payment is called piecework. Jobs that paid by the hour were very rare.

Cesar and his family worked in all the California valleys, picking such crops as grapes, apricots, onions, and walnuts. They also picked cherries, cantaloupes, cabbage, cotton, broccoli, peas, carrots, and beets.

During the Chavezes' travels, they encountered farms where the workers were on *strike* for better pay or for better working conditions.

The Chavez family never crossed the *picket lines,* no matter how much they needed the money. Cesar's father became a member of many of the unions that were trying to organize the farm workers. Librado strongly believed in treating every person fairly and always stood up for himself and others.

When his father was hurt in a car accident, Cesar left school in the eighth grade and went to work full-time in the fields. He had planned to complete his education after a couple of years of work, but that was not to happen.

Like many teenagers, Cesar went through a stage of rebellion. He liked modern music and dressed *pachuco*, which means "flashy" in Spanish. Pachuco was a style very popular with Mexican Americans in the barrios: They wore their hair long—in a ducktail—and sported tapered pants, long coats, keychains, and broad hats.

In the fall of 1942, 15-year-old Cesar and his friends went to a little malt shop in the barrio. There Cesar met a girl who was wearing flowers in her hair. Her name was Helen Fabela, and it was not long before Cesar and Helen began to date. Six years later, Cesar and Helen got married.

In 1944, during World War II, Cesar served in the U.S. Navy as a deckhand, mostly on small ships. Once, when he and some navy friends from Texas were on leave in Delano, California, they decided to go to the movies. In those days many buildings were segregated, which meant that there were separate sections reserved for whites only, even in movie theaters. Cesar felt that because he was serving his country, he deserved to sit anywhere he wanted. The theater management did not agree, so Chavez and his friends were arrested for breaking the rules.

Although he was later released, Cesar Chavez would remember this act of discrimination. Discrimination is the unfair treatment of an individual, group, or race. Chavez was angry about the way with which he was dealt, but he did not yet know how to lead the fight against this kind of injustice.

Cesar Chavez (second from right) became an organizer for the Community Service Organization (CSO) in 1952. The CSO worked to improve the farm workers' way of life.

3

A Beautiful Part of Life

Cesar Chavez waited to give the signal to his friends, who had gathered in his house, that would tell them to get up and throw the man out. Chavez thought the man would be another *gringo*, which is an unflattering term used by Mexicans to describe white North Americans. The only whites that Chavez had seen coming into the barrio were policemen or social workers. Social workers are employed by the government to visit the poor to provide services to people who need economic aid or help in adjusting to the community. Many people in the barrio, including Chavez, did not believe that the social workers served the needs of the community very well.

But the tall, thin Fred Ross, dressed in well-worn clothes, seemed to talk about things that mattered. Ross spoke quickly and directly to the men in Chavez's living room on that June evening in 1952. He spoke about the many problems of Sal Si Puedes. For instance, the stream behind the barrio carried waste from a nearby packinghouse. The children who played in the stream got sick with sores. Mosquitoes bred in the stagnant pools, but the authorities did nothing to get rid of the pests. Cesar Chavez listened as Ross spoke of how poor people could establish power for themselves to put pressure on the authorities to solve these problems. "He did such a good job of explaining how people could build power that I could even taste it, I could *feel* it," Chavez later told a biographer, Peter Matthiesen.

Fred Ross, an organizer for the *Community Service Organization (CSO)*, was working to help Mexican Americans throughout California. After Ross finished speaking to the people in Chavez's home that night, Chavez walked with him to his car.

"I have another meeting now," Ross said. "I don't suppose you'd like to come?"

"Oh, yes, I would!" Chavez replied. He was very excited. At last someone was offering him a way to put his thoughts about helping others into action. His feelings about equality and justice for farm workers could now be channeled into something that actually had a name and a direction—community service. Chavez later said that meeting Fred Ross had changed his life. Ross was equally excited about meeting Chavez. That very first night, Ross wrote in his diary: "I think I've found the guy I am looking for."

Another person who helped shape Chavez's awareness of organizing against social inequality was Father Donald McDonnell. Father McDonnell was the only priest who would come into Sal Si Puedes to conduct church services.

CSO organizers Hiram Samaniego (left), Cesar
Chavez, and Fred Ross (right) review plans in 1952.
Upon meeting Chavez, Ross immediately recognized
his talent for helping people.

Chavez helped him with odd jobs, and they soon became good friends. They had long talks about the problems of farm workers and the migrant labor system. Father McDonnell also explained the economic side of growing crops. He introduced Chavez to the biographies of St. Francis of Assisi and Mohandas K. Gandhi. St. Francis was a 13th-century Italian monk who devoted himself to helping the poor. Gandhi was the leader whose philosophy of using *nonviolence* to achieve social change helped India attain its independence in 1947.

In Gandhi's deeds Chavez saw the effectiveness of his own mother's dichos. He realized that great men were those who set a good example. Gandhi's philosophy became very important to Chavez, and he felt that the CSO could be an effective way to make nonviolent changes in the farm workers' way of life.

The CSO had two main programs—voter registration and citizenship classes. Chavez immediately volunteered, working every night for two months on a registration drive. Soon the CSO hired him full-time. Chavez watched Ross and learned about organizing meetings in people's houses and pressuring city officials for fair voting rules. Chavez later described his own organizing work during that time as a beautiful part of his life.

He spoke at meetings in people's homes and went door-to-door to get them involved in activities to help their community. When Fred Ross was sent to another town, Chavez became the leader of the local registration drive in Sal Si Puedes. By election time in 1952, the CSO had registered 6,000 new voters.

Chavez proved to be a natural leader, and people felt comfortable coming to him with their questions. He took the time to help them with their problems, not just with voter registration, but also with government agencies, such as the welfare board and the immigration department.

He even helped them with their day-to-day problems at the doctor's office and at school.

From these experiences, he learned two valuable lessons. The first was that helping others cost him very little, personally, and it rewarded him enormously. "One night it just hit me," he recalled. "Once you helped people they became very loyal. The people who helped us . . . were the people we had helped."

The second lesson Chavez learned was that government agencies and officials were more likely to listen to someone who had the power of people's votes behind him. He explained one of the keys to his success in bargaining by saying, "I seldom like to go see my opponent, unless I have some power over him."

Chavez's work for the CSO took place mostly in the cities. He preferred living in the country, however, and wanted to become more involved with the migrant workers' struggle. In August 1958, Chavez finally got his wish. He and his wife, Helen, and their seven children moved to the farming community of Oxnard, California, where he was to begin organizing a CSO chapter.

At Chavez's first CSO meeting in Oxnard, a man asked him angrily, "Why is it we cannot get jobs? The *braceros* have all our jobs. What are you going to do about that?" (Braceros are migrant farm workers from Mexico.)

Chavez was stunned. He thought the big issue among the people would be how they could make the unguarded railroad crossing safer. Chavez remembered that several Mexican-American children, including one of his school friends, had been killed there.

Yet in house meeting after house meeting, the issue of the braceros came up first. Because of a labor shortage during World War II, a special government program allowed U.S. growers to bring Mexicans into the country to work on their farms. At one time, Oxnard had a bracero labor camp that held 28,000 workers.

One of the rules of the program, however, stated that braceros could not be used if local labor was available for the job. Yet the local workers complained to Chavez that braceros were hired before they were.

This was the difficult issue that Chavez decided to tackle. Fighting the injustice meant that farm workers would have to oppose other farm workers, that the Mexican Americans would have to challenge Mexicans. Chavez, however, was not bothered by the touchy undertaking. "There's an old dicho," he explained. "You cannot exchange one God for another. This was a question of justice, and I've never had any problem making a decision like that."

Chavez's first task was to find out why no one could get work. The next morning he got up early and applied for work at the bracero camp. The people in charge sent him to the Farm Placement Service, eight miles away, to get a referral slip. The office opened at 8:00 A.M. When he returned to the camp with the necessary papers, it was too late. The workers had been dispatched to the fields at 4:00 A.M., so the next morning Chavez showed up at 4:00 A.M.

"I am sorry," the contractor told him. "I cannot send you because this referral slip is out-dated. It is yesterday's." *That* was the problem. The system of hiring required a referral slip, but the slip prevented local workers from getting the job. The growers were then able to pay the braceros lower wages. Barely earning enough money on which to exist, the braceros had to pay room and board to the growers, even for the days there were no jobs. "The braceros were poor when they came," Chavez said, "and were poor when they went back."

Chavez felt that ending the bracero program would be the best course of action for everyone. Others had complained about the problems with the program, but no one could prove that it was unfair. Chavez planned to use the Farm Placement Service's own rules to show how corrupt the program had become. By logging each of his visits to the placement office on a separate file card, he hoped to get enough records to have proof of the unjust rules.

Every day, in the fall of 1958, Chavez applied for work, and when he was turned down he kept a record of it. Little by little, others joined him, and they all went down to the placement office to fill out the forms.

During this period, Chavez met with the Farm Placement Service's officials and the U.S. Department of Labor, trying to get them to end the bracero program. When nothing was done to change the situation, Chavez began to put pressure on the local store owners. He passed out leaflets that stated, "Dear Mr. Merchant, the reason we do not buy here is because the growers will not let us work. They have braceros working, and they take all the money to Mexico."

Meanwhile, his idea of getting proof to show the authorities caught on. Two hundred workers per day were crowding into the Farm

Placement Service to fill out forms. Chavez kept a record of each application, until he had 1,900 cards. He then gave 10 referral cards to the man in charge of the program and asked him why these men could not get work. The man began to sweat nervously. "There are a lot of complaints here," he protested. Chavez gave him 60 more cards.

After 3 weeks, when the man could not come up with reasons for the lack of jobs, Chavez gave him another 100 cards. The pressure Chavez and the workers were putting on the state government started to get results. The federal government decided to investigate the Farm Placement Service. Eventually the head of the organization was fired for taking bribes.

The growers finally agreed to hire people at the CSO office instead of at the bracero camps so that local workers could get jobs. Chavez also wanted the growers to guarantee the workers' rights, but the CSO did not want Chavez to become involved in starting a labor union.

For his successful work in Oxnard, Cesar

Chavez was appointed national director of the CSO and was transferred to Los Angeles. He had won an important victory. For the first time, the farm workers had fair hiring practices and decent wages. But the joy of victory did not last long.

When Chavez went back to Oxnard six months later, the braceros were back at work and the CSO chapter had fallen apart. Another organization had taken over, and the rivalry between that organization and the CSO had destroyed the new system.

Despite the need Chavez had found for farm work projects such as the one he had begun in Oxnard, the CSO's 1961 national convention voted against starting a similar labor project elsewhere. They said the CSO was a civic, or citizen's, organization, not a labor organization. Chavez disagreed. He felt that poor people could help themselves only if they could get decent jobs— the real need of the migrant workers. Chavez stood up in front of everyone. "I have an announcement to make," he said. "I resign."

Cesar and Helen Chavez are pictured here with seven of their eight children after they returned to Delano, California. Some of the children are holding the National Farm Workers Association's flag: a black eagle in a white circle on a red background.

4
Birth
of a Union

Written on the ceiling in the bedroom, directly above him where he could not miss seeing it, was the name Paul. Chavez was so busy forming his union, attending meetings, and making phone calls that he had very little time to be with his family. Paul, his 12-year-old son, was reminding Chavez that he was needed at home.

But during 1961, Chavez was needed *everywhere*. Moving back to his wife Helen's hometown in Delano, California, Chavez began to organize farm workers to form a union. It was a difficult task. Helen went to work picking grapes 10 hours a day to support the family while Chavez went into the fields to sign up workers. He covered 14,867 miles in 86 days; picking peas and grapes, meeting with more than 2,000 migrant workers—in dusty fields, on dirt roads, and in the tiny living rooms of their barrio homes. Many people thought he was crazy, trying to do so much with so little money. Others believed in what he was doing—his brother Richard; his cousin Manuel; and Dolores Huerta, a former CSO organizer—all gave up their jobs to join him.

Slowly, the union, which was called the National Farm Workers Association, grew. The NFWA offered a credit union (a kind of savings program for workers by which they could make deposits and get loans), life insurance, community service programs, and a buyer's cooperative that sold goods to its members at a discount.

The union held its first convention in an abandoned movie house in Fresno, California, on

September 30, 1962. Cesar's brother Richard designed a union flag that would become their symbol: a black eagle in a white circle on a red background. They adopted the slogan Viva La Causa (Long Live the Cause).

In the spring of 1965, the union had its first *huelga*, or strike. When employees strike, they stop working in order to get better conditions on the job. The NFWA had prepared carefully in order to make sure the strikers would get what they wanted. Huerta and Chavez went to the homes of all the members on the first morning of the strike, making sure that everyone stayed home. They were striking against the Mount Arbor Company, growers of rosebushes. Rose grafting is hard work, requiring a lot of skill. Workers crawl along the bushes to insert rosebuds into slits they make in the stalks. The smallest mistake will mean the bud will not grow and the bush will be no good. Rose grafters were promised $9.00 for every 1,000 plants they spliced, but they were getting paid only about $6.50.

Labor contractors ignored the strike and brought workers from other farms. Because rose grafting is such highly skilled labor and the new workers could not perform the task as well, the growers agreed to give the striking workers a raise, only four days after the strike began.

To Chavez's small union it was a victory, and the union attracted many new members who had heard about it. Feeling confident and proud, Huerta and Chavez continued to sign up new members.

On September 7, 1965, Chavez and the NFWA were unprepared for an event that put their union to the test. Grape pickers—laborers who do another job that requires skilled hands and knowledge—walked out at Lucas and Sons vineyard. The grape strike quickly spread throughout the valley. Chavez did not feel his union was strong enough to handle a big strike yet. The NFWA had 1,200 members, but only 200 paid dues. Still, if they were a union, their members could not cross a picket line. The union held a rally on September 16 to call its members together to decide whether to strike. Chavez made an appeal to the members that they should keep the strike nonviolent or have no strike at all. When he asked if they agreed, the members roared back, "Yes!" They could not have known then, but the grape strike was going to last five long years.

Chavez and his union boycotted the growers' products to make it more expensive for the growers to handle a strike than to pay the farm workers a decent wage.

5

Boycott Grapes

During a protest march from Delano to Sacramento, the capital of California, Chavez's right ankle swelled to the size of a melon. The sole of his left foot became one huge blister. A high fever and bad back caused him constant pain. Nevertheless, Chavez led hundreds of striking grape pickers on a march in 1966 to call attention to their demands.

The striking grape pickers had been replaced on the farms by *scabs*, an unflattering name for people who take jobs away from the workers who are on strike. Striking workers, who are called pickets when they walk a picket line, were arrested or threatened with violence. Chavez understood that picketing alone would not be enough to win their demands. What the union needed was to make it more expensive for the growers to deal with a strike than to pay their workers a fair wage.

One of the ways to accomplish this was to *boycott*. A boycott is an act of protest. An organization urges consumers not to buy from, use, or deal with certain companies or stores. Chavez's idea was to target the growers that were large companies rather than to try to boycott all the growers. He knew that if a big company negotiated with the union, smaller companies would soon follow. The big company he chose was Schenley, a wine and liquor manufacturer. Chavez's union supporters handed out flyers urging people not to buy Schenley products. The NFWA picketed the dockyards in San Francisco. In support of the strikers, the International Longshoremen's and Warehousemen's Union refused to load the scab-picked grapes onto the boats.

The boycott hurt Schenley's sales. Two days before the march reached Sacramento, a Schenley manager called Chavez and said the company would sign a contract with the strikers. The march ended on Easter Sunday, 1966, on the steps of the capitol. Before a crowd of more than 10,000 people, Cesar Chavez announced that an agreement for a contract had finally been reached.

The giant DiGiorgio Corporation was the NFWA's next target. It had tens of thousands of acres of grapes and thousands of acres of pears, plums, and apricots throughout California and 5,000 acres of citrus fruit in Florida. The Di-Giorgio Corporation also owned S & W Fine Foods, TreeSweet Products, several processing plants, and a sawmill.

The corporation was known for its anti-union stand, and it had broken at least three attempted strikes in the past. The company got a court order limiting the number of pickets the NFWA could have on the picket line during the strike. The court order made it hard for the union to stop the scabs from working. Some NFWA members called for the use of violence. A discouraged Chavez searched for another way to win support for their cause. Three women approached Chavez and asked him: If they held a mass across the street from the farm, would the judge arrest them? Chavez realized that this plan might be the perfect way to have lots of people show their support of the workers without needing hordes of pickets.

The next morning, outside DiGiorgio's gates, union members began holding prayer services. Scab workers came out at lunchtime to pray and to talk to the striking workers about their cause. They soon signed up with the NFWA. To Chavez the gathering was a wonderful example of the power of nonviolence.

The NFWA's supporters in Chicago, San Francisco, and New York set up a boycott of DiGiorgio's products. When DiGiorgio realized how much the boycott could hurt the company, it agreed to hold elections for a union. But the vote was not only for whether the workers wanted a union but for *which* union they wished to represent them. The company preferred the Teamsters Union, a very powerful national union that many people think is corrupt and has ties to organized crime. Chavez believed that the Teamsters and the growers would work out a deal between themselves to help each other and not the workers. He also thought the Teamsters and the growers had tampered with the election results, enabling the Teamsters to win.

The NFWA had been getting moral and financial support from the American Federation of Labor and Congress of Industrial Organizations (AFL-CIO), another national union. With the AFL-CIO's help, the NFWA convinced the state labor board that new elections were necessary. Then it decided to join the ranks of the AFL-CIO. The new name of Chavez's union officially became the *United Farm Workers (UFW)* in 1972.

Eventually, the UFW won the right to represent the workers in the election. But there was another problem. Some growers were loaning their brand names to other growers that the union was boycotting. Because the union was boycotting only certain brands, a grower could switch the labels and then sell its grapes under the new label.

Chavez decided to try to prevent the growers from switching labels. He declared a boycott on all California grapes. College students and labor unions across the country set up picket lines outside supermarkets and grocery stores asking people not to buy California grapes. Senator Robert Kennedy of New York and other politicians expressed support for the boycott. All over the country, people stopped buying California grapes. The publicity helped make the nation aware of Cesar Chavez and the migrant workers' struggle.

But for some of the striking workers, with families to feed, events were not moving fast enough. Sheds were burned down on several farms, fights broke out on picket lines, and some pickets began to carry guns. To stop union members from using physical force to do harm, Chavez called a union meeting and announced that he was discouraged by the way the workers were handling the strike. He felt that there were no shortcuts to their goals and that violence would bring failure. He declared that he would begin a *fast*, that he would not eat any food, until the violence stopped.

For 25 days Cesar Chavez did not eat. He was weak and his friends worried about his health. His weight fell from 175 to 140 pounds. When Chavez's fast finally ended on March 10, 1968, Senator Robert Kennedy and 4,000 people came to celebrate mass with him in a Delano park. Cameramen and reporters crowded around as Reverend Jim Drake read the words Chavez had written but was now too weak to speak: "Our struggle is not easy. . . . But we have something the rich do not own. We have our own bodies and spirits and [the] justice of our cause as our weapons."

Then, in front of the television cameras,

Senator Robert Kennedy gives Chavez a piece of bread during a mass on March 10, 1968. Chavez fasted to stress the religious and nonviolent nature of the farm workers' strike against California's grape growers.

Senator Kennedy gave a piece of bread to Chavez. "The world must know," Kennedy said, "that the migrant farm worker, the Mexican American, is coming into his own right."

The symbol of the Mexican-American farm worker became the black eagle of the UFW. If a package of grapes did not have the black eagle on it, people all across the country refused to buy it. Grape growers were losing so much money that on July 29, 1970, the largest growers signed contracts with the UFW. The strike had finally ended.

Cesar Chavez had no time to celebrate the victory. The next day the San Francisco newspapers announced that 80 percent of the growers in the Salinas area had signed 5-year contracts with the Teamsters Union. The details, including wages, working conditions, and health benefits, were to be worked out later. These growers were the ones that produced most of the nation's lettuce, strawberries, and vegetables that are grown in rows. The growers and the Teamsters had met in secret to negotiate union contracts that were favorable to the growers. Chavez's union would have to start its work all over again, this time with the lettuce growers.

Three of the largest growers were big companies: InterHarvest, Pic 'N Pac, and Freshpict. InterHarvest farms were owned by United Fruit, whose parent company, United Brands, imported Chiquita brand bananas. Freshpict Corporation, growers of lettuce and other crops, was owned by Purex, which was a household name in laundry bleach. Pic 'N Pac, owned by the S. S. Pierce Company, was the largest strawberry grower in the world.

The UFW now turned its boycott from grapes to lettuce—and any of the products sold by the companies that grew lettuce. It was hoped, for example, that many consumers would stop buying Purex bleach or Chiquita bananas. The big companies worried about what effect the boycott would have on them. They were soon willing to sign contracts with the UFW. But the Teamsters Union already had the contracts and would not release the growers from them. The Teamsters tried to force the UFW, and Cesar Chavez, to give up organizing the row-crop workers by using violence.

Jerry Cohen, Chavez's lawyer and friend, was badly beaten by a farm owner and some Teamster thugs. Pickets were attacked on the picket line. Someone planted a bomb outside the UFW's headquarters. The Teamsters threatened the UFW and some of the growers as well. When InterHarvest became the first to sign a contract with the UFW, the Teamsters would not let InterHarvest trucks leave the parking lot. They also stood across the street and threatened the drivers with baseball bats and rocks.

Most of the growers did not want a union at all. The Bud Antle lettuce growers obtained a court order against the UFW, stopping the boy-

In 1970, UFW lettuce workers go out on strike in Salinas, California. The union called a strike to protest the growers' contracts with the Teamsters Union.

cott. Chavez believed that the court order was illegal, so he ignored it and was soon arrested. He knew the trial would help bring national attention to the lettuce boycott. Chavez's lawyers expected to win the case. They were shocked when the judge sentenced Chavez to jail.

In December 1970, farm workers keep up a 24-hour vigil across the street from the jail in which Chavez was being held. Chavez was arrested for ignoring a court order to stop the lettuce boycott.

During the lettuce boycott, Chavez had been working constantly. He was under a great deal of pressure and was in poor health. A doctor who visited Chavez while he was in jail ordered a special diet to build up his strength. Throughout December 1970, farm workers kept a constant vigil outside his jail cell. Union lawyers worked continually to free Chavez, and finally, on Christmas Eve, Chavez was released. Four months later, the California Supreme Court ruled that the original court order opposing the lettuce boycott was against the law.

Several lettuce growers finally sat down with the union to negotiate a deal that would recognize the UFW and release them from the Teamsters' contracts. During these meetings, U.S. Treasury agents gave Chavez some chilling news—an informer had come to them and told them that there was a plot to murder him. Somewhere, they did not know where, a man who had a notch in his right ear and who wore a tattoo that read Born to Lose was waiting to kill Chavez.

In 1986, Chavez squeezes a bunch of grapes at a rally in New York City to boycott grapes. Chavez and the UFW protested the use of poisons in pesticides, which are unhealthy for the farm worker and the consumer.

CHAPTER

6

The Labor Camps

W hen a poor person got into his car, Joe Brown would pull out a gun and force that person to become his slave. Poor people, attracted by Joe Brown's offer of a job, were kidnapped by him and paid as little as two to five dollars a week to work for him. He forced them to live in his labor camp in Florida; sometimes, three people had to live together in one tiny room. He drove them to town to register for food stamps; then he took the food stamps, bought food, and sold it back to the poor people for the little money that they had earned from their work.

One of the UFW workers had discovered Brown's practice while organizing a union in Florida. Brown, who was a labor contractor, had 29 farm laborers working like slaves. In 1973, when he was finally arrested for his ill treatment of the workers, he had $45,000 in cash and drove a custom-built Cadillac.

The news of the arrest and the horrible living conditions at the labor camp appeared in every newspaper in Florida and in many papers throughout the country. Robert Washington and Theodore Johnson, two of the farm workers at the camp, agreed to testify in Tallahassee against a bill that had been introduced in the state legislature. The proposed bill would prevent the use of farm worker hiring halls in Florida. Chavez and the UFW had previously worked hard to permit the use of hiring halls when they were organizing in California. The Florida hiring system depended on labor contractors, such as Joe

Brown, who handpicked workers themselves, regardless of experience or ability. They never told the workers how much money they would actually be paid. Chavez and his union wanted to explain to the state legislature that hiring halls established rules by which farm workers could get jobs fairly, without discrimination.

Coca-Cola's Food Division was one of the UFW's biggest supporters. It had previously signed a contract that improved the living conditions in its Florida labor camps. The company was so pleased with the UFW that its workers actively campaigned against the bill to outlaw hiring halls. The bill was being powerfully pushed by the growers.

During the 1973 hearings, the public learned that the drinking water in most of the labor camps in Florida was harmful. They also learned that the health department had known about the impurity for years. But when the public found out that the drinking water in Miami Beach was just as unhealthy, state officials finally did something to make the water safe to drink. At the same time, the UFW started a letter-writing campaign to tell about the injustices at the labor camps. After discovering the polluted water and learning the details about the Joe Brown case, the Florida legislature voted to defeat the anti–hiring halls bill.

Meanwhile, the man whom the U.S. Treasury agents thought was going to kill Chavez had been captured and sent to prison for murdering someone else.

Things were beginning to improve for Chavez and the UFW, until they received news that when the UFW contracts with the grape growers of California expired, the growers were going to sign contracts with the Teamsters.

Chavez and the UFW tried to make the growers understand that the union's interests were not against theirs. They told them that farm workers wanted to join the UFW and not another union. But the growers would not listen to him, and they signed a contract with the Teamsters.

The contract took away the workers' hiring hall and their grievance procedure—the process by which they could make formal complaints about unsatisfactory working conditions. The agreement also eliminated the laborers' pesticide protection. The pesticide protection clause was important for the workers because, in the past, they had to work in the fields right after the crops had been sprayed with poisons to kill pests. Many workers had fallen ill from the poisons. The UFW had to call off its lettuce boycott and return to boycotting grapes.

Some of the Teamsters used violence against the farm workers, and the growers tried to use the courts against the pickets. Many pickets were arrested and put in jail, including Chavez's daughter, Linda. The Teamsters kept up a pattern of violence against the UFW pickets. Several fights broke out, a picket was shot in the shoulder, and a farm worker's trailer was burned down. The nation's largest winery, Gallo Brothers, signed up with the Teamsters and then tried to evict 70 UFW families and their children from the labor camp. Some of these families had worked at Gallo for as long as 14 years.

In August 1973, two UFW members had been killed during the conflict. Despite the two deaths, Chavez stuck to his principle of nonviolence. "If we had used violence," Chavez told Peter Matthiessen, "we would have won contracts long ago, but they wouldn't be lasting, because we wouldn't have won respect."

Finally, in 1975, the Agricultural Labor Relations Act was passed in California. It benefited both agribusiness and the UFW. It was the first law ever passed for farm workers in the United States. The law created an Agricultural Labor Relations Board to oversee labor practices and to supervise union elections on the farms. Fifty-three percent of the farm workers voted for the UFW during the election, and only 30 percent voted for the Teamsters. The struggle between unions was over, but the conflict with the growers persisted.

Chavez (left) and Dolores Huerta (center) explain the dangers of pesticides to a television reporter in Fresno, California.

In San Diego, California, Chavez (second row, far left) joins hundreds of Union-Tribune employees and actor Ed Asner (first row) in a 1990 boycott against a controversial labor contract.

CHAPTER

7

The Ongoing Struggle

Vineyards surround the villages scattered throughout California's valleys. To anyone who drives through these towns, they appear to be sleepy, peaceful farm communities. But to those who live in the towns, they have an atmosphere of fear: There is a constant concern of getting cancer from the pesticides that are sprayed on the area's crops. Scientific studies made in the valleys have found that some of these towns have higher numbers of cancer victims than do other areas.

In 1987, Cesar Chavez and the UFW decided to call attention to the danger of pesticides by declaring another major boycott of grapes. The Environmental Protection Agency had claimed that five poisons used in pesticides might be harmful to the farm workers' health, but the growers continued to use the poisons.

In 1988, to protest the use of the pesticides and to make people more aware of the farm workers' problems, Chavez went on another fast, this one lasting 36 days. Near the end of the fast, the widow and children of Senator Robert Kennedy were at Chavez's side to show their support, just as Kennedy himself had done 20 years before.

The UFW had hoped that the California Agricultural Labor Relations Board would help change many of the injustices faced by the farm workers, including low wages, poor living conditions, and lack of medical insurance. Many UFW members do not believe that the board has been as successful as was originally hoped. Many in the union believe that the board's members,

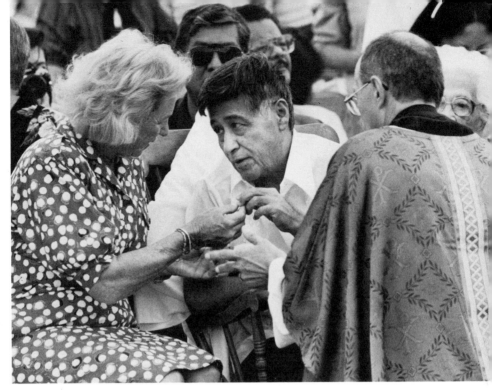

On August 21, 1988, Chavez receives a piece of bread from Ethel Kennedy, ending his fast protesting the use of pesticides.

who are appointed by the state governor, have sided with the growers too often. They also allege that growers have found ways to avoid negotiating with the UFW—for example, table-grape growers never again signed contracts with the farm workers, even though the workers voted for the UFW.

In February 1990 Chavez leads an anti-parathion protest in Sacramento, California. Parathion is an extremely poisonous insecticide.

Despite the many setbacks, Cesar Chavez, as president of the United Farm Workers, remains the guiding force behind the union. His wife, Helen, their eight children, and his children's children are all actively involved in union activities. Chavez lectures at colleges and universities across the United States, explaining the farm workers' struggle to each new generation.

To relate the story of Cesar Chavez is to recount the story of all farm workers. He has dedicated his life to helping others, sharing the dream of a better life that his grandfather had more than 100 years ago. In addition to better pay for farm work, the UFW has brought new dignity and respect to Mexican Americans. Furthermore, Chavez and his co-workers accomplished this goal without resorting to the use of violence.

In spite of the unending hard work—and the long way he has yet to go to achieve fair treatment of all farm workers—Chavez is not discouraged. One of the dichos that Chavez likes to repeat is: "Hay más tiempo que vida" (There is more time than life). He once commented, "We don't worry about time, because time and history are on our side." Cesar Chavez devoted himself to others, to fighting injustice in a completely non-violent way. History will remember him as a great man who by his example led the farm workers on the path to equality.

Further Reading

Other Biographies of Cesar Chavez

Day, Mark. *Forty Acres.* New York: Praeger, 1971.

Franchere, Ruth. *Cesar Chavez.* New York: Crowell, 1970.

Roberts, Naurice. *Cesar Chavez and La Causa.* Chicago: Children's Press, 1986.

Terzian, James P., and Kathryn Cramer. *Mighty Hard Road: The Story of Cesar Chavez.* Garden City, NY: Doubleday, 1970.

White, Florence M. *Cesar Chavez, Man of Courage.* Champaign, IL: Garrard, 1973.

Related Books

Freeman, Richard. *What Do Unions Do?* New York: Basic Books, 1984.

Graves, Charles Parlin. *Robert F. Kennedy, Man Who Dared to Dream.* Champaign, IL: Garrard, 1970.

Chronology

March 31, 1927   Cesar Chavez is born on a farm near Yuma, Arizona.

1937–44   Chavez and his family travel throughout California as migrant farm workers.

1944–46   Serves in the navy during World War II as a deckhand.

1948   Marries Helen Fabela.

1952   Meets Fred Ross and begins working for the Community Service Organization (CSO).

1962   National Farm Workers Association (NFWA), organized by Chavez, holds first convention in Fresno, California.

1965   NFWA begins strike against California grape growers that lasts five years.

1966   Chavez attracts the attention of Senator Robert F. Kennedy, who investigates the strike; NFWA calls off grape boycott of Schenley Industries after signing the first

contract for farm workers in the
United States.

1968   Chavez goes on a fast in protest of
the violence of the strike; ends fast
after 25 days at a mass with
Senator Kennedy and 4,000 people.

1970   Strike officially ends on July 29,
after agreement with grape
growers; Chavez and NFWA
protest the Teamsters Union's
involvement with lettuce growers;
Chavez sent to jail for refusing to
call off lettuce boycott.

1972   NFWA is granted a charter by the
AFL-CIO and changes name to
United Farm Workers (UFW).

1975   State of California passes the
Agricultural Labor Relations Act,
the first bill of rights for farm
workers.

1988   Chavez fasts for 36 days to protest
the use of pesticides and to draw
attention to the problems of farm
workers.

1991   Travels to colleges and universities
throughout the United States
lecturing on the farm workers'
struggle.

Glossary

agribusiness a company's involvement in the growing, buying, selling, and supplying of agricultural products

boycott an act of protest in which the public is urged to stop buying from or dealing with a store or company in order to force the store or company to meet certain demands

Community Service Organization (CSO) a private California-based group created to organize the poor in order to get the authorities to change bad conditions and to improve their community

fast to go without all or certain foods for a period of time for religious reasons or as a form of protest

labor contractor a person who serves as a middleman between the growers and the farm workers; the contractor provides laborers to the grower, and the grower pays the contractor, who in turn pays the laborer for the work

migrant worker a laborer who travels from one farm to another, planting or harvesting different crops

National Farm Workers Association (NFWA) the first union that Cesar Chavez organized in California to improve the working conditions of farm workers

76

nonviolence a form of protesting without using physical force to obtain certain goals, such as recognition or government assistance

picket line a group of people posted by a labor union at a business that is affected by a strike; strikers who walk a picket line are called pickets

scab an insulting term for a person who takes the job of a worker who is on strike

strike the stopping of work by laborers in order to get better working conditions

United Farm Workers (UFW) the name given to Chavez's union when it was granted a charter by the AFL-CIO in 1972

Index

Bruce W. Conord is a graduate of Rutgers University and is a freelance writer. His articles have appeared in several newspapers and magazines, including the *Trenton Times* and *American History Illustrated*. He first became aware of the migrant workers' struggle as a child, when he visited the labor camps of blueberry pickers and saw their poverty firsthand. Mr. Conord lives in Hightstown, New Jersey, with his wife, two dogs, and a cat.

Picture Credits